Why Wasn't I Enough?

And Other Questions About Affairs

Jeffrey D. Murrah

Restore The Family Press

Contents

Chapter One

Why Wasn't I Enough?

Asking, *'Why wasn't I enough?'* cuts deep. It's a heart-wrenching question that haunts many of us after being cheated on.

Imagine you're sitting across from the person you love, your heart heavy with this unspoken question: *'Why wasn't I enough?'* You're searching their face for any sign of the love you once shared, wondering how it all slipped away. You start questioning yourself and the relationship.

Let's take a look at the question and responses to it.

First, it is a "Why?" question. Why questions are looking for explanations. By their very nature, you put people on the defensive when you use "Why?" questions. These questions have an accusatory tone to them. These questions also focus on the past. They look at what happened and try to find the answers in the past.

They look for who or what to blame. Even the addition of "Wasn't" in this title focuses on the past. This question puts both the questioner and the party being questioned under scrutiny. Both are on emotional trial.

When you use the question *"Why Wasn't I Enough?"*, you seek explanations for inadequacy. It also assumes that the party being cheated on was inadequate. It's heartbreaking, really. This question stems from a place of feeling not good enough, which couldn't be further from the truth.

Each time you replay those moments, the silence feels heavier, and the air around you grows colder, leaving a bitter taste of confusion and sorrow.

Such questions carry the baggage of assumptions with them. By posing these questions to the cheater, you give them an easy out. It assumes something is wrong with you, and all they have to do is identify some traits or qualities you lack to answer the question. It is a question from the language of inadequacy. You want to know the faults and start pointing the finger of blame at yourself.

The answer is most likely that nothing is wrong with you. The problem lies with the cheater and their choices.

Instead, you might find it more healing to ask yourself, "*What needs to be added to our relationship?*" or "*What more do you need from me or us?*"

Since most cheaters often act without thinking through their choices, they probably cannot identify the real issues. The cheaters that do think frequently obsess about a few qualities to justify their cheating activities. They focus on one or two faults and use those as their excuse. It's as if they have a standard mantra they say whenever you question them. They also have a highly inflated value on sexual activity and selfishness. It is as if they want to act out sexually and are looking for an excuse.

Fault-finding is a way to identify and excuse. They use fault-finding like a "get out of jail free card" to avoid the pain of their choices. In this case, you give them an easy out by assuming something was wrong with you.

Understanding the Journey of Healing

Healing from an affair is not a linear process; it involves navigating through various stages of grief, anger, and acceptance. Acknowledging your feelings without judgment and understanding that healing takes time is important.

Patience with yourself is paramount. Recognize that it's okay to have good days and bad days.

The Importance of Self-Compassion

Self-compassion is critical during this time. Treat yourself with the same kindness and understanding you would offer a dear friend in a similar situation. Self-blame can be a common reaction to being cheated on, but it's essential to remember that the infidelity was not your fault. The choices made by the cheater were theirs alone.

Engaging in Self-Care Practices

Self-care is vital for emotional recovery. It encompasses a wide range of activities that nourish both your body and mind:

Physical Activity: Exercise can be a powerful tool in managing stress and improving mood. Find a physical activity you enjoy, whether it's yoga, running, or dancing, and make it a regular part of your routine. A healthy diet is also important since it impacts your mental health and ability to think clearly.

Healthy Diet: Eating healthy regularly is critical. When you quit eating or skip meals, your body and brain do not have the energy or nutrients they need to function well. Not eating or eating poorly puts your thinking in a "fight, flight, or freeze" reactionary mode.

Mindfulness and Meditation: These practices can help center your thoughts and reduce anxiety. Even a few minutes a day can significantly impact your overall well-being.

Creative Outlets: Engaging in creative activities such as writing, painting, or playing music can be therapeutic. It allows you to express your feelings in a constructive and personal way.

Social Support: Lean on friends and family for support. Sharing your feelings with trusted individuals can provide comfort and perspective.

Professional Help: Sometimes, the guidance of a therapist or counselor can be invaluable in navigating through the complexity of emotions and decisions post-affair.

Rebuilding Self-Esteem

The blow to self-esteem following an affair is significant. Rebuilding self-esteem involves:

Affirmations: Practice positive affirmations that reinforce your values and strengths.

Some examples are:

1. **Self-Worth Affirmation**: "I am enough, just as I am. My worth is not defined by someone else's actions or choices. I deserve love and respect, and I commit to treating myself with kindness and understanding every day."

2. **Strength and Resilience Affirmation**: "I am strong, resilient, and capable of overcoming challenges. This experience does not define me. I choose to grow and learn from it, embracing my journey towards healing and self-discovery."

Setting Boundaries: Learn to set healthy boundaries in relationships. This can help you regain control and respect in your interactions. When setting boundaries, it is important to write them down and begin each one with "I will..." or "I will not..."

Here are two boundary examples:

1. **Communication Boundaries Example**: "I will regularly have open and honest conversations about our feelings and relationship. However, these discussions must be respectful and constructive. If the conversation becomes accusatory or we feel overwhelmed, we agree to pause and revisit the discussion when we're both calmer. This ensures we're addressing issues without causing additional hurt." Another way of putting it is that "I will be honest and open in conversations. I will not hide my true feelings to avoid hurting others. If things get too heated, I will take a break."

   This boundary sets clear expectations for communication, emphasizing the need for respect and the importance of managing emotions during sensitive conversations. It acknowledges the potential for emotional distress while creating a space for constructive dialogue.

2. **Personal Space and Privacy Boundaries Example**: "I will maintain my personal space and privacy." While rebuilding trust is crucial for us moving forward, I also believe in the importance of maintaining personal space and privacy. We agree to respect each other's personal devices, social media, and individual time. If concerns about trust arise, we commit to discussing them openly rather than resorting to snooping or invading each other's privacy. Trust must be rebuilt on mutual respect and understanding, not surveillance.

   This boundary addresses the delicate balance between rebuilding trust and respecting personal privacy. It recognizes the natural concerns about trust after an affair but emphasizes that respect and open communication are the keys to healing and rebuilding the relationship.

Celebrating Small Wins: Acknowledge and celebrate your achievements, no matter how small. This can help rebuild confidence and a sense of self-worth.

Finding Joy Again

Rediscovering joy and happiness after an affair is crucial. Pursue activities and hobbies that bring you pleasure. Allow yourself to explore new interests or revisit old ones you may have neglected. Finding joy in the small things can gradually lead to a more profound sense of fulfillment and happiness.

Embracing Vulnerability in Conversations

Opening up a dialogue about an affair requires immense courage and vulnerability. It's like walking on a tightrope, where every word could either bridge the gap between you and your partner or widen it. So, how do you start these conversations without falling into the pit of accusations and defensiveness?

Imagine sitting down with your partner, the air heavy with unsaid words. Instead of launching into a "Why?" that might make them retreat into a shell, try saying, "I've been feeling disconnected from us lately, and it hurts. Can we talk about what we both need to feel closer again?"

This approach acknowledges your feelings without placing blame, setting the stage for an open dialogue.

Crafting Questions That Open Doors

Questions that start with "Why?" often shut down conversations before they begin. They're like doors slamming shut. But when you reframe these questions, you're gently knocking, inviting your partner to open up.

Instead of asking, "Why did you do this?" consider asking, "What led us to this point?" This doesn't excuse their actions but seeks to understand the dynamics that contributed to the situation. It's a way of saying, "I'm here to listen, even if it hurts."

Active Listening: The Heart of Communication

Active listening is crucial. It's about fully concentrating on what's being said rather than passively hearing the speaker's message. Focus on what is said rather than your mind's interpretation.

Picture this: your partner is sharing their thoughts, and instead of planning your next argument, you pause, digest their words, and respond with, "I hear you saying that you felt neglected. Is that right?" This validates their feelings and encourages a deeper level of sharing.

Navigating Emotions Together

Remember, emotions will run high. There's no doubt about it.

There will be moments when anger, hurt, or frustration bubble up, threatening to derail the conversation. When this happens, take a deep breath and express your emotions without blame. Say, "I'm feeling really hurt right now, and I need a moment to process this."

It's okay to take breaks during these discussions. The goal isn't to resolve everything in one sitting but to build a bridge back to each other, one honest conversation at a time.

Setting Boundaries for Future Conversations

Finally, setting boundaries for how you'll communicate moving forward can help prevent future heartache. This might look like agreeing to weekly check-ins about your relationship or promising to speak up sooner when you're feeling unhappy. It's about creating a safe space for both of you to express your needs and desires without fear of judgment or retaliation.

By approaching communication with empathy, openness, and a willingness to listen, you can navigate the aftermath of an affair with grace and compassion. Remember, it's not about finding the perfect words but creating a space where both of you feel heard, valued, and understood.

Chapter Two

Why Do Single Women Actively Seek Married Men?

The Complex Dynamics of Single Women Attracted to Married Men

Why are some single women drawn to married men? This question opens a complex chapter on human desires, societal norms, and the intricate web of relationships. At first glance, it might seem like a straightforward issue, but the reality is anything but simple. The motivations for a single woman seeking the companionship of a married man vary widely, challenging many common assumptions.

Understanding the Motivations

The heart of this exploration lies in understanding the varied motivations that lead some single women down this path. Research by John Jacobs has shed light on four main factors influencing attraction: distress, identity enhancement, aging and social pressure, and sexual desires. These factors are universal in relationships, yet they manifest uniquely when single women are attracted to married men.

Distress as a Catalyst:

For some, a married man represents a way out of a stressful situation or status, viewed as a safer option, especially if he refuses to leave his spouse. This perceived safety can often lead relationships to evolve from platonic to sexual, sometimes intentionally, other times not.

In such cases, both parties are using the other for convenience. Although the married man may legitimately be trying to help a maiden in distress, the help becomes sexualized and turns into something else. In some cases, the sexualizing of the relationship is accidental; in some cases, it is intentional.

Seeking Identity Enhancement:

Another reason is the allure of completing one's identity through another. The myth behind this one is that the married man will "complete me." Married men, especially those in positions of power or influence, like pastors or professors, are seen as adding value or meaning to a woman's life, fulfilling a potential that seems otherwise out of reach.

Aging and Social Pressure:

The fear of becoming a spinster, combined with the ticking of the reproductive clock, drives some women toward married men as a way to circumvent these pressures. Society also plays a role, filling the void left by a spouse's death or divorce with expectations to find a new partner. The amount of social pressure varies with culture, with some cultures exerting tremendous pressure on the single female.

The Role of Sexual Desires:

In an age of sexual liberation and performance-enhancing drugs, sexual desires become a strong motivator. The pursuit of sexual fulfillment, driven by various factors, including physical attraction and the thrill of the new, can lead to unexpected connections.

A close cousin to sexual attraction is romantic attraction. In such cases, the single woman needs the emotional stimulation that sex or romantic involvement brings. This is where issues such as sexual addiction and love addiction come into play. Like a drug addict, they go from relationship to relationship, seeking a buzz. Such people only feel like themselves when they are at the heightened levels of stimulation that such romantic and sexual liaisons provide.

Security and Self-Esteem in Unconventional Relationships

In my conversations with individuals navigating the complex terrain of relationships, two additional motifs frequently emerge, veiling deeper emotional landscapes: the quest for security and the pursuit of self-esteem.

The Quest for Security

One poignant narrative shared with me illuminated the deliberate choice of a single woman to make connections exclusively with married men. This decision wasn't rooted in the pursuit of love or long-term companionship but in a strategic move toward stability without the weight of commitment. She sought the company of someone who could offer financial free-dom and the exuberance of shared experiences without nudging toward marriage.

In her eyes, this arrangement provided a fortress of security, a safeguard against the vulnerabilities accompanying deep emotional entanglements. This form of relationship became her sanctuary, allowing her to experience intimacy while keeping the complexities and expectations of a traditional partnership at arm's length.

The Pursuit of Self-Esteem

Another compelling aspect that surfaced was the intricate dance with self-esteem. For some, the allure of engaging with married men lies not in the depth of connection but in the thrill of competition and its validation. Winning the affections of someone else's partner is seen as a testament to their desirability, an ego boost that transcends mere attraction. There is a thrill to beat out another woman. This conquest becomes a mirror reflecting their worth and attractiveness back at them, serving as a tangible measure of their appeal. These interactions, though fleeting and fraught with moral ambiguity, offer them a momentary high, a reassurance of their allure in the eyes of others.

Moral and Ethical Considerations

While exploring the reasons behind these unconventional relationships, addressing the moral and ethical implications is crucial. Engaging in a re-lationship with a married man involves a breach of trust and commitment, not only for the individuals directly involved but also for the unsuspecting spouse and family. The potential for emotional and psychological harm to all parties is significant, and the consequences are far-reaching.

Societal and Cultural Factors

Societal norms and cultural expectations further complicate the dynamics of these relationships. In many communities, the stigma attached to being a single woman, especially as one age, can be overwhelming. The stigma increases in intensity with age. The pressure to find a partner can be intense, even if it means compromising one's values. Additionally, in some cultures, the power dynamics between men and women can make it more challenging for single women to assert their autonomy and make healthy relationship choices.

Navigating the Complexities

For single women who find themselves drawn to married men, it's essential to take a step back and examine the underlying emotional needs and desires driving these attractions. Seeking professional help, such as therapy or counseling, can provide a safe space to explore these issues and develop healthier coping mechanisms. Cultivating a strong sense of self-worth and independence and recognizing that true fulfillment and happiness come from within, not from external validation or relationships.

Real-Life Experiences

To illustrate the complexities of these relationships, let's consider the story of Sarah, a successful professional in her mid-30s. Sarah was attracted to her married colleague, Mark, who seemed to offer the emotional support and attention she craved. Despite knowing the moral implications, Sarah pursued the relationship, convincing herself that Mark's unhappy marriage justified her actions. In some ways, she believed she was saving him. She wanted to see him happy. This desire to help him turned into an affair. However, as the affair progressed, Sarah found herself consumed by guilt and anxiety, realizing that she was compromising her own values and potentially causing harm to Mark's family.

Final Thoughts

The attraction of single women to married men is a complex and multifaceted issue rooted in a range of emotional, psychological, and societal factors. While the motivations behind these relationships may vary, it's crucial to recognize the potential for harm and the importance of making healthy, ethical choices. By understanding the underlying drivers and seeking support, single women can navigate these challenges and find fulfillment in relationships that align with their values and goals.

Security and self-esteem unveil the multifaceted reasons some single women engage with married men. Beyond the surface-level explanations lie deep-seated needs and desires, ranging from the practical to the psychological. Understanding these motivations demands empathy and a willingness to explore the intricate weave of human relationships, where each story holds its unique shades of complexity.

Chapter Three

How Do I Kill the Feelings of a Forbidden Affair?

How to End an Affair and Heal from the Emotional Aftermath

You've been carrying the burden of this secret for far too long, and it's eating away at you from the inside. Deep down, you know it's time to end the affair, but the thought of untangling yourself from this mess feels overwhelming.

Affairs are a lot more common than people think. Research shows that around 1 in 5 married couples will face infidelity at some point. When it happens, it sends shockwaves through a relationship. Both partners are left reeling, trying to make sense of the betrayal and pick up the pieces.

If you're ready to end your affair, you're probably feeling all sorts of mixed emotions right now. It's scary to think about closing the door on something that's become such a big part of your life, even if you know it's wrong. You might feel pulled in two directions, torn between the feelings you developed for your affair partner and your commitment to your primary relationship.

Acknowledging the Depth of the Challenge

The heart of the matter lies in recognizing that what you're attempting to do is not merely ending a relationship but letting go of a part of yourself. The connections formed during the affair and the emotions it stirred have woven themselves into your very being. To extricate these feelings is to undergo a process of self-renewal.

The Roadmap to Emotional Liberation

The Final Goodbye:

Begin by unequivocally ending the affair. This isn't a 'see you later' episode but a decisive conclusion to this chapter of your life. You will need to end the affair with the real person and the image of that person in your head. Killing off the feelings is not easy. It often feels like you are killing part of yourself, which you are.

The attachment and bonds that formed and their associated feelings have become a part of you. The attachments and feelings will need to be severed, both inside of you and between you and the lover. It may also take 6-18 months for the feelings to fade. As more time goes by, the intensity of the feelings will diminish as long as those feelings are not romanticized or fantasized about. Replace those feelings by nurturing a healthier relationship with your spouse.

The pathways formed in your brain associated with the affair need to be overpowered and replaced by the relationship with your spouse.

Confront Your Feelings:

Honesty is your ally on this journey. Lay bare the emotions the affair stirred within you - lust, excitement, companionship, and anything else that surfaces. Writing these down can provide clarity and serve as the first step towards understanding and overcoming them.

As part of the process, you may need to write them down, regardless of whether or not they make sense. For example:

- lust

- companionship

- excitement

- feeling alive

- selfishness

- young

- ???

Trace the Roots:

Understanding where these feelings stem from is crucial. They could be echoes of past relationships or desires for what once was. Recognizing these origins is essential for moving forward. Although most people are unaware of their inner thoughts, emotions, or processes, gaining that awareness is required to overwrite their influence in your life.

It is hard to kill feelings if you do not know their origin. You will want to take them out, roots and all. If your lover reminds you of someone or at some other time, acknowledge it. If your lover reminds you of your spouse when they were younger, admit it.

Since our choices reveal much about our needs, honesty about where these feelings originate will tell a great deal about your needs. The lover may be an 'idealized' or 'romanticized' version of what you seek. Use this time to learn about yourself.

Mind, Heart, and Soul Alignment:

Pinpoint where these emotions reside within you. If they linger in your thoughts, challenge and change them. If they clutch at your heart, reset your emotional compass. This alignment is pivotal for transformation.

Are these feelings coming from your head, heart, gut, or elsewhere? This step may require effort since people often react without thinking or considering where things are coming from.

This is an important part of the process of self-honesty. Depending on where the sensations are coming from, you will be alert to what steps to take to deal with them.

You can change your thoughts if your feelings are coming from your head. You can start by "fast-forwarding" your mind to where giving in to this feeling will lead and considering whether your response is based on facts or fantasies.

Heart-based feelings can be changed with some re-adjustment to your willpower and time. Since the heart is reactive, you may need to change what it is reacting to. If your heart wants something, try to identify what it is about your lover that your heart is reacting to. Is it their voice, their walk, their look, etc.? This will let you fine-tune the focus of your heart.

Eradicate Triggers:

Remove any physical reminders of the affair from your life. This step is about creating a space that supports your emotional recovery rather than hinders it. Changing your environment can significantly impact your healing process.

This step involves removing the reminders of that person from your life. Cards, knick-knacks, photos, etc., must be removed and thrown away. These can become triggers that elicit reactions that you are trying to remove. This also includes no longer listening to the songs associated with the affair partner, avoiding places the two of you went to, and not visiting the restaurants where you ate. These can be triggers that activate a flood of feelings.

Adjust Your Environment:

This extends beyond just removing reminders. Alter your daily routines, change your surroundings, and create new patterns that don't include the affair or the person. It's about building a new normal that supports your growth and healing.

In the recovery community, people talk about "changing playmates, playgrounds, and play toys." You will need to apply this to your situation as well. Change your routine, change the furniture arrangement, change the pictures on the wall. Leaving things as they were can also trigger old feelings.

Navigating the Impact on Your Primary Relationship

Ending the affair is only the first step in the healing process. It's crucial to address the impact on your primary relationship and work towards rebuilding trust and communication with your partner.

Be prepared for a range of emotions from your partner, including anger, hurt, and betrayal. They may have questions about the affair and need time to process their feelings. It's essential to be open, honest, and patient during this process, even if it's painful. They may also need to discuss the affair and its impact often. Work with them on those issues. Taking the 'once and done' approach to talking about the affair is a mistake. They will need to talk about it several times.

The Importance of Professional Support

Ending an affair and dealing with the complex emotions that come with it can be overwhelming. Don't hesitate to seek professional help, such as individual therapy or counseling, to support you through this challenging time.

A therapist can provide a safe, non-judgmental space to explore your feelings, develop coping strategies, and work on personal growth. They can also help you navigate the impact on your primary relationship and provide guidance on rebuilding trust and communication.

Forgiveness and Self-Compassion

Forgiveness is a crucial part of the healing process, both for yourself and for your affair partner. It doesn't mean condoning the affair or forgetting the pain it caused, but rather letting go of the anger and resentment that can keep you stuck. That anger and resentment may be toward your spouse, affair partner, or someone else.

Remember to be compassionate with yourself during this time. Everyone makes mistakes, and healing requires being kind to yourself. Acknowledge that you are human and that you are doing your best to make amends and move forward.

Potential Challenges and Setbacks

The process of ending an affair and healing from its impact is not always linear. There may be moments of weakness, setbacks, or lingering emotions. This is a normal part of the journey and doesn't mean you've failed. It is often a two-step forward, one-step backward, one-step sideways progression. Such detours are a normal part of making changes.

If you find yourself struggling, seek support from a trusted friend, family member, or therapist. Remember that healing takes time, and it's okay to have setbacks along the way.

Learning from the Experience

While an affair is a painful experience, it can also be an opportunity for growth and self-reflection. Take the time to examine the factors that led to the affair within yourself and your primary relationship.

Use this experience as a catalyst for personal growth and strengthening your relationship with your partner. Consider what you've learned about yourself, your needs, your communication style, and how to apply these insights moving forward.

Resources for Further Support

If you're seeking additional guidance and support, consider exploring the following resources:

- Books on healing from infidelity, such as "After the Affair" by Janis A. Spring or "Not Just Friends" by Shirley P. Glass

- Support groups for individuals recovering from an affair, such as Beyond Affairs Network (BAN) or Infidelity Survivors Anonymous (ISA)

- Online resources and forums, such as SurviveYourPartnersAffair.com, SurvivingInfidelity.com or AffairRecovery.com

Remember, you don't have to navigate this challenging time alone. Reach out for the support and resources you need to heal and move forward.

When used consistently, these steps will reduce, if not kill, the feelings. Since some feelings do not die easily, reducing their intensity may require time. However, if you give in to them, the feelings will continue increasing until they are uncontrollable.

Ending an affair and healing from its impact is a challenging but necessary process. You can work towards emotional liberation and personal growth by following the steps outlined above, seeking professional support, and practicing forgiveness and self-compassion. Remember, healing takes time, but with commitment and support, moving forward and creating a new, healthier chapter in your life is possible.

Chapter Four

Why Do Men Cheat if Their Woman is "Doing What She's Supposed To?"

Why Some Partners Cheat Despite a Seemingly Good Relationship

The recovery community uses sayings and catchy phrases that contain wisdom in a pithy format. Because they deal with hurting people on a daily basis, they have developed an awareness of human nature.

One such saying concerning infidelity is, "No one leaves a good lover except a sex addict."

This phrase provides valuable insight into human behavior and gives clues about where to look for possible answers when infidelity occurs in a seemingly good relationship.

However, it's essential to approach this topic with empathy and understanding, acknowledging that infidelity is a complex issue with multiple contributing factors beyond just sexual addiction.

The Complexity of Infidelity

While the saying "No one leaves a good lover except a sex addict" suggests that sexual addiction may play a role in some cases of infidelity, it's crucial to recognize that there are many factors at play. These can include emotional disconnection, unresolved relationship issues, individual mental health struggles, or a misalignment of needs and expectations within the relationship.

It's important to avoid oversimplifying the issue or blaming only one partner. Instead, approaching the situation with empathy and a willingness to understand each partner's perspective can be more productive in addressing the underlying issues.

The Role of Individual Responsibility

While it's valuable to explore the potential reasons behind infidelity, it's crucial to emphasize that the decision to cheat is ultimately the responsibility of the individual who engages in the behavior. Regardless of the state of the relationship or any personal struggles, each person is accountable for their choices and actions. The cheater made the decision to use adultery as their solution to the issues they are facing.

This isn't to say that the betrayed partner is without fault or that their actions didn't contribute to the state of the relationship. However, it's essential to distinguish between relationship issues that need to be addressed and the decision to engage in infidelity as a response to those issues.

Relationship Expectations and Communication

The phrase "doing what you're supposed to do at home" can be problematic, as it suggests a one-size-fits-all approach to relationships. What one considers "doing what they're supposed to" may not align with their partner's needs or expectations.

Instead of relying on assumptions or societal norms, partners must communicate openly and honestly about their individual needs and expectations within the relationship. This involves vulnerability, active listening, and a willingness to work together to find a mutual understanding. Although each spouse should talk about their needs and expectations, they often don't talk about their sexual and emotional needs or their expectations in those areas. In such cases, the spouses assume that their partner should know those things.

It often surprises me that couples will be able to discuss their sexual fantasies more easily than their sexual fears and needs. If you and your partner have never had an in-depth discussion about your needs and expectations, this is an opportunity to start that conversation. Approach it with curiosity, empathy, and a desire to understand each other better.

The Impact of Infidelity on the Betrayed Partner

While understanding the reasons behind infidelity is important, it's equally crucial to acknowledge the profound emotional impact on the betrayed partner. The discovery of an affair can be traumatic, leading to feelings of betrayal, hurt, anger, and a loss of trust. Although the cheater may not have intended for the hurt or damage, they now have to face the reality that damage was done.

If you are the betrayed partner, know that your feelings are valid and that healing is possible. Seek support from trusted friends, family members, a minister, or a therapist who can help you process your emotions and develop coping strategies. It is important to share your story and feelings rather than keeping them inside or making assumptions about those experiences.

If you are the partner who engaged in infidelity, it's essential to take responsibility for your actions, including the unintended impact of your choices, and be willing to do the work necessary to rebuild trust and repair the relationship if that is the path you and your partner choose. This often means you need to initiate the discussions about the affair.

Addressing Sexual Addiction and Past Experiences

If, after honest communication and self-reflection, you discover that sexual addiction may be a factor in your relationship, it's important to approach the issue with compassion and a commitment to healing. Sex and Love addictions often have shame associated with them for both spouses. Rather than shaming and condemning each other, consider seeking treatment options to deal with those issues.

Sex and love addictions are serious issues requiring support and ongoing work to address. It's crucial to separate the person from their behavior and to approach the situation as a team, working together to address the addiction and rebuild the relationship.

It's also important to recognize that past experiences, such as a history of sexual abuse, traumas, or family patterns of infidelity, can contribute to an individual's behavior. However, these experiences do not determine a person's choices or excuse hurtful behavior. Healing from past traumas and learning healthier coping mechanisms is crucial for personal growth and the health of the relationship.

Chapter Five

Who Are They Having an Affair With?

Uncovering the Hidden Meaning Behind Your Partner's Choice of Affair Partner

When you discover that your partner has been unfaithful, it's natural to focus on the pain of betrayal and the logistics of what happens next. Your mind races ahead, thinking through every possible scenario. However, taking a closer look at the person your partner chose to have an affair with can provide valuable insights into the underlying issues and unmet needs that may have contributed to the infidelity. Consider both similarities and dissimilarities in appearance, attitude, and behavior. These things will provide clues to understanding your spouse's inner world.

The Surprising Similarities

One of the most striking things you might notice when looking at your partner's affair partner is that, in some cases, there is a resemblance to yourself. Consider how much they resemble you physically or in terms of personality and interests. This similarity can be painful and confusing, leaving you wondering, "If they want someone like me, why not just be with me?"

It's important to understand that these similarities reveal a deep love for you, even if your partner has difficulty expressing or fully embracing that love in the present. The choice of an affair partner who resembles a younger, more idealized version of you may indicate a longing for the passion and connection that characterized the early stages of your relationship.

For example, Susan found herself reeling when she discovered that her husband, Mike, was having an affair with a woman who looked remarkably like her, just ten years younger. As she grappled with feelings of betrayal and inadequacy, Susan realized that Mike's choice revealed a desire to recapture the spark and excitement of their early years together before the stresses of work and family life had taken their toll. Once she saw this, she knew what was needed in her relationship.

The Role of Unmet Needs

While the similarities between you and the affair partner can be striking, it's crucial to recognize that attraction is a complex interplay of various factors. Your partner's choice of affair partner may also reveal unmet emotional or psychological needs that they are attempting to fulfill outside of the primary relationship.

These unmet needs can take many forms, such as a desire for validation, excitement, or emotional connection. For instance, John, a successful businessman, was drawn to his vibrant and adventurous co-worker, Lisa, despite being married to his high school sweetheart, Emily. Through therapy, John realized that his attraction to Lisa stemmed from a deep-seated fear of missing out on life's adventures and a longing for the spontaneity and passion he felt was lacking in his marriage.

Recognizing the role of unmet needs in your partner's choice of affair partner can be a challenging but essential step in the healing process. By identifying and addressing these needs together, you and your partner can work towards building a stronger, more fulfilling relationship.

In John's case, more spontaneity and passion were needed. He and Emily could work on improving this.

The Impact of Past Experiences

Another factor that may influence your partner's choice of affair partner is their past relationships and experiences. Unresolved issues from childhood or previous relationships can shape an individual's attachment style and emotional needs, unconsciously guiding them toward partners who fill a familiar role.

For example, a successful attorney, Charlotte found herself repeatedly drawn to unavailable men, including her married colleague, David. Through self-reflection and therapy, Charlotte recognized that her attraction to unavailable partners mirrored her childhood experience of an emotionally distant father. By working to heal these old wounds and develop a more secure attachment style, Charlotte broke the pattern of attraction and built healthier relationships. As she explored these issues, the intensity of her attraction decreased. She no longer needed their attention.

Bonds formed earlier in life can impact one's decisions now. The greater the intensity of the bond, the greater its influence. Those bonds can be either positive or traumatic in origin, although the trauma bonds are the most troublesome.

The Path to Healing

Once you've taken the time to understand the factors that may have influenced your partner's choice of affair partner, the next step is to use this insight to facilitate healing and strengthen your relationship.

This process begins with honest, open communication. Encourage your partner to share their perspective on what drew them to the affair partner, and listen with empathy and an open mind. It is also important to listen to them without interrupting them. Share your observations and insights, and work together to identify areas where your relationship may have been lacking. Let them know what you see, along with the emotions it brings.

It's also important to remember that healing from infidelity is a gradual process that requires patience, commitment, and often the support of a qualified therapist, counselor, or minister. By working through the underlying issues and developing new ways of connecting and meeting each other's needs, you and your partner can emerge from this challenging experience with a stronger, more resilient bond.

Chapter Six

The Wrong Questions

Asking the Right Questions to Save Your Marriage

When you suspect or discover that your marriage is in trouble, it's easy to get caught up in a whirlwind of emotions and distractions. You might ask questions like, "What does a counselor cost?" "What does a private eye cost?" or "How much does a divorce attorney cost?" But these are the wrong questions to focus on when your relationship is on the line.

Take the story of Carol and Jacob. When Carol discovered that Jacob had been having an affair, her first reaction was to look up the cost of hiring a divorce attorney. She spent hours researching legal fees and reading reviews, all while her heart was breaking and her marriage was crumbling. It wasn't until a close friend asked her, "But what do you really want, Carol? Is divorce truly the answer?" that she realized she had been asking the wrong questions all along. The questions you ask yourself shape your thinking and where you look for answers. Asking the wrong question will give you an answer, albeit not one that helps heal your marriage.

The Right Questions

Instead of getting caught up in the financial or logistical aspects of a troubled marriage, ask yourself the questions that truly matter:

- What are the underlying issues in our relationship that led to this point?

- Have I played a role that contributed to the current state of our marriage?

- What steps can we take to rebuild trust and connection?

- How can we prioritize our relationship and make it stronger than ever before?

These questions are challenging to consider, but they will ultimately lead you toward healing and growth.

The story of David and Sarah will help illustrate this issue. When Sarah found out about David's infidelity, she was tempted to react with anger and impulsivity. But instead, she took a deep breath and asked herself, "What do I really want for our future? Is there a way to rebuild what we once had?" By focusing on the right questions, Sarah and David were able to have honest conversations, seek counseling, and ultimately strengthen their bond.

Misplaced Priorities

One reason couples often ask the wrong questions when facing infidelity or a troubled marriage is misplaced priorities. In today's fast-paced, materialistic world, it's easy to get caught up in pursuing success, wealth, or status while neglecting the relationships that truly matter. The questions you ask focus your attention and priorities. They determine the direction your marriage takes.

Let me illustrate with Michael and Lisa. They had been married for ten years, but their connection gradually faded. Michael always worked late at the office, while Lisa focused on maintaining their perfect home and social image. When Lisa discovered that Michael had been confiding in a female coworker about their marital problems, she was shocked and felt threatened. But as she reflected on their priorities, she realized they had both been putting their energy into the wrong things.

Lisa faced the decision of either directing her anger at Michael and the co-worker or taking steps to re-prioritize her marriage. One choice aimed to remove the threat, and the other would improve her marriage. You may be facing choices similar to those Lisa made.

Taking Action

When your marriage is in trouble, the most important thing is to take action. Don't let fear, vulnerability, or uncertainty hold you back from addressing the real issues in your relationship.

Start by having an honest conversation with your partner. Share your feelings, concerns, and hopes for the future. Listen to their perspective with an open mind and heart. Strengthen your marriage before lashing out at others or asking the wrong questions. Together, plan how you will make your marriage relationship a priority and work towards healing.

Consider seeking the support of a qualified therapist, minister, or counselor who can guide you through this challenging time. Remember, investing in your emotional and relational health is just as important as investing in your physical health or material possessions.

Tanya and Robert knew their marriage was in trouble when they started sleeping in separate bedrooms and avoiding each other's company. But instead of letting their relationship deteriorate further, they made the brave decision to seek couples counseling. Through that experience, they learned how to talk with each other, address past hurts, and rediscover the love and connection that had brought them together in the first place. It took several tries, yet they managed to have regular times that they talked with each other. Through those talks, they discovered they needed to incorporate more play in their marriage to pull together. They realized they had each been looking out for number one rather than prioritizing their relationship. They forgot to have fun like they did when they were dating. Although their friends told them to take care of 'themself,' they had not considered the importance of keeping playfulness and fun in their marriage.

Focus on what truly matters. And take action to build the strong, loving, and resilient marriage each of you deserve. With time, effort, and an open heart, you can emerge from this challenging chapter stronger and more connected than ever before.

Chapter Seven

The Danger of Making Excuses

Confronting the Hard Truths About Affairs

Imagine this: a respected pastor, known for his inspiring sermons and moral leadership, stands before his congregation and admits to having an affair. His justification? "It was a form of anxiety reduction." The words hang heavy in the air, a flimsy excuse for a profound betrayal of trust.

But this pastor is not alone. Affairs occur in many families and across all professions, from the highest government offices to the most modest homes. And with each affair comes a litany of excuses, a desperate attempt to rationalize the unforgivable. Excuses are made to rationalize what happened. The cheater may give lip service to doing wrong yet use excuses to make it sound like they did it for the right reasons.

The Pervasiveness of Affairs

It's easy to assume that affairs are rare, something that happens to other people in other places. But the truth is far more unsettling. Studies have shown that infidelity occurs in up to 40% of marriages, cutting across all demographics and social strata.

From the charismatic CEO who claims his affairs are a necessary release from the pressures of his job and the perks of his position to the stay-at-home parent who justifies their infidelity as a response to feelings of neglect, the excuses are as varied as they are hollow.

The Psychology of Making Excuses

So why do people feel the need to make excuses for their behavior? At its core, it's a way to avoid taking responsibility for one's actions. By shifting the blame to external factors—stress, loneliness, and a lack of fulfillment—individuals can maintain a sense of their own goodness and morality. They want to view themselves as either good people or having good intentions.

When making excuses, the person makes it sound like they did what they did for the right reason. What they consider the right reason may vary from love to purpose to feeling alive again. In making excuses, they often avoid considering the consequences of their choices.

But this is a dangerous game. When we make excuses, we deny ourselves the opportunity for growth and change. We become trapped in a cycle of self-justification, unable to confront the painful truths about our choices and their consequences.

The Role of Power and Privilege

The temptation to make excuses can be especially strong for those in positions of power and privilege. When you're used to getting what you want, it's easy to feel entitled to break the rules, to believe that the normal standards of behavior don't apply to you. Some cheaters view themselves as 'above the rules.' In their mind, their special status gives them special privileges.

We see this play out in the halls of government, where elected officials caught in scandals often resort to blaming their indiscretions on the pressures of public life. We see it in the boardrooms of corporations, where high-powered executives justify their affairs as a perk of their position. They may view themselves as 'special' in a way that morals and rules do not apply to them.

But power and privilege are not a license to behave badly. If anything, those who hold positions of influence have a greater responsibility to model integrity and accountability.

The Consequences of Affairs

Regardless of the excuses made, the consequences of affairs are devastating. They shatter trust, destroy families, and leave deep emotional scars that can take a lifetime to heal.

For the individuals involved, the fallout can be severe. Feelings of guilt, shame, and self-loathing are common, as are anxiety, depression, and even thoughts of suicide. Relationships with partners, children, and friends may be irreparably damaged, and the reputation one has worked a lifetime to build can be ruined instantly.

By making excuses, the cheater sends the message that their version of events is what is most important. This attitude devalues their spouse. When the excuse is believed wholeheartedly, it gaslights their partner, leaving them wondering what the truth is.

Chapter Eight

The Tangled Web of Denial and Lies in Infidelity

Infidelity is a storm that leaves devastation in its wake, shattering trust and dismantling the very foundation of a relationship. At the heart of this tempest lie secrets, denial, and lies – a complex tapestry that ensnares both the adulterer and the betrayed spouse in a cycle of pain and confusion. These can become so prevalent that the cheater believes their own lies or the betrayed believes the gaslighting statements directed at them.

The Secrets That Bind

To illustrate, imagine a married couple, Sarah and David. They seem like the perfect pair – happy, successful, and deeply in love. But beneath the veneer of their picture-perfect life, David harbors a secret: he's been having an affair with his coworker, Brenda.

As David navigates the murky waters of his double life, he becomes increasingly entangled in a web of secrets. He lies to Sarah about his whereabouts, feelings, and intentions. He creates elaborate stories to cover his tracks, always one step ahead of the truth. David believes he is smart or clever enough to craft a believable story.

But secrets have a way of festering, eating away at the very fabric of a relationship. And when Sarah stumbles upon a suspicious text message on David's phone, the carefully constructed house of cards begins to tumble. David initially remains true to his story. He denies the evidence, even suggesting that Sarah is paranoid and imagining things.

These kinds of scenarios are common when it comes to affairs.

The Protective Cloak of Denial

Denial is a powerful force in the face of infidelity. For Sarah, the initial response is to deny the signs that have been staring her in the face. The late nights at the office, the unexplained absences, the emotional distance – she tells herself it's all in her head, that David would never betray her.

But why do we deny when the truth is so painfully clear? For Sarah, denial serves as a protective shield to stave off the overwhelming emotions that come with the realization of betrayal. It's a coping mechanism to maintain a sense of control in the face of chaos.

For David, denial takes on a different form. He denies the severity of his actions, telling himself that the affair is just a harmless fling and that "it doesn't mean anything." He denies the impact of his choices on Sarah, convincing himself that what she doesn't know won't hurt her. He does not consider that his claim of the affair not meaning anything diminishes his own marriage.

The Lies We Tell Ourselves

But denial is not the only tool in the adulterer's arsenal. Lies, both to oneself and to others, play a crucial role in perpetuating the cycle of infidelity. David lies to Sarah, to his friends, and to his family. He creates a facade of normalcy while living a double life. It takes hard work to keep his two worlds apart.

But perhaps the most insidious lies are the ones we tell ourselves. David tells himself that he deserves the affair and that he's entitled to happiness outside of his marriage. He tells himself that the affair is a result of Sarah's shortcomings, that she drove him to seek solace in another's arms. He further justifies his action by thinking he deserves to be happy. In extreme cases, David-like characters tell themselves that "God wants him to be happy."

These lies serve a purpose—they allow David to justify his actions and shirk responsibility for the pain he's causing. They enable him to maintain a sense of self-righteousness, even as he betrays the very person he vowed to love and cherish. He is putting his own happiness ahead of everyone else.

The denial not only concerns the affair but also includes David denying the good parts of his marriage to Sarah. He denies the good times they shared and the common vision they had.

Navigating the Road to Healing

When the truth of David's affair finally comes to light, Sarah is left reeling. She feels betrayed, angry, and utterly lost. How can she ever trust David again? How can she rebuild a relationship so thoroughly shattered by deceit?

The road to healing is long and arduous, but it begins with a commitment to honesty—with oneself and one's partner. For Sarah and David, this means having difficult conversations and confronting the painful truths that have been buried beneath layers of denial and lies. The lies have to be exposed for what they are.

It means taking responsibility for one's actions, including lying, expressing remorse, and being willing to do the hard work of rebuilding trust. It also means that he has to come face to face with how his lies have impacted Sarah and others. Healing is not just a matter of confessing the lies; it requires the cheater to make things right as well.

Even when David starts being honest, it may take several months for him to be honest before Sarah starts believing him again. During that time, she may be questioning where he goes, who he's with, and when he'll be home repeatedly. She needs the reassurance that she can believe what he is telling her before she is willing to show trust towards him again.

Forgiveness and Acceptance

Perhaps most importantly, healing requires forgiveness—not just of one's partner but of oneself. Sarah must learn to forgive David, not for his sake but for hers. She must let go of the anger and resentment that threaten to consume her to make space for the possibility of a new beginning. What he did was wrong. Forgiveness is not about condoning the affair, it is about letting go of the pain and the desire for revenge.

David must also learn to forgive himself, accept responsibility for his actions, and commit to being a better partner and a better person. He must learn to embrace honesty, even when it's painful, and trust in the power of vulnerability. Being vulnerable and honest is not easy. It carries with it the risk of being hurt, embarrassed or shamed.

Initially, they will need to practice overcommunication until Sarah can believe David. For David, this amounts to him developing a habit of telling the truth. This includes the truth about his activities, feelings, and financial matters. If there are any areas in which he begins hiding information, the old habit of lying and denial could grow again.

The two of them will also need to practice acceptance of each other the way they are. This includes practicing unconditional love toward each other.

Chapter Nine

Should I Spy on Him/Her?

Navigating the Minefield of Infidelity Suspicions

Imagine this: you're going about your day when a nagging feeling starts to creep in. Something doesn't feel quite right in your relationship. Your partner is suddenly more secretive, their phone is always face down, and they're working late more often than usual. The suspicion of infidelity begins to take root, and you find yourself wondering, "Should I spy on them?"

It's a question that many people grapple with when faced with the gut-wrenching possibility that their spouse is cheating. The desire for answers, for certainty in the face of doubt, can be all-consuming. But before you go down the rabbit hole of surveillance and secret-gathering, it's important to consider the potential consequences.

The Double-Edged Sword of Spying

On the surface, spying on your spouse may seem like the quickest path to the truth. After all, if they're not being faithful, there will be evidence, right? Text messages, emails, mysterious receipts – the breadcrumbs of betrayal.

But the reality is rarely so clear-cut. Whether through technology or a private investigator, spying can open up a Pandora's box of legal and ethical issues. Your spouse has a right to privacy, and depending on your methods, you may be crossing legal boundaries in your quest for answers. You can find yourself facing legal problems with spying.

More than that, spying can take a heavy toll on your own emotional well-being. Imagine the constant anxiety of checking your partner's every move, the sleepless nights spent poring over their browser history, the sinking feeling in your stomach every time their phone buzzes. Is this really how you want to live?

The Cracks in the Foundation

Beyond the personal toll, spying can also have a devastating impact on your relationship. The very act of spying implies a lack of trust, and once that trust is broken, it is incredibly difficult to repair. Even if your suspicions are unfounded, the fact that you felt the need to spy can create a rift between you and your partner that may be impossible to bridge.

And if your spying does uncover evidence of infidelity? Your betrayal may be compounded by the guilt of violating your partner's privacy. You may question their actions and your own – was spying the right choice? Did two wrongs make a right?

A Path Forward

So, what can you do if you suspect your spouse of cheating but don't want to resort to spying? The first step is to have an honest conversation with your partner. Express your concerns and allow them to respond. This can be a difficult and painful conversation, but it's crucial for getting to the root of the issue.

You may need to present your evidence, suspicions, and how it impacts you. Bear in mind that some spouses will come clean while others deny any wrongdoing and may even turn things around and accuse you of not trusting them. Address the distance that has developed between the two of you and ways of decreasing that distance.

It's also important to prioritize self-care during this challenging time. Lean on your friends and family support system, engage in activities that bring you joy and relaxation, and don't be afraid to seek professional help if you're struggling to cope.

The Bottom Line

At the end of the day, the decision to spy on your spouse is a deeply personal one. There is no one-size-fits-all answer, no easy solution to the pain of suspected infidelity.

But before you take that step, ask yourself: What do I hope to gain from spying, and at what cost? The answers to these questions may help guide you towards a path of healing, whether that means working to rebuild your relationship or making the difficult decision to walk away.

Remember, you are not alone in this struggle. Countless others have stood where you stand and have felt the same anguish and uncertainty.

So take a deep breath, trust your instincts, and remember: the truth has a way of coming to light, even in the darkest times. You have the strength to face whatever lies ahead - and the wisdom to know that sometimes, the greatest act of love is to love yourself first.

Chapter Ten

Is He/She Cheating?

Reading Between the Lines: Navigating the Uncertainty of Suspected Infidelity

The Gut-Wrenching Reality

Picture this: you're in a relationship that you thought was rock-solid. You've built a life together, shared your hopes and dreams, and faced challenges as a united front. But lately, something feels off. Your partner is distant and secretive, and their behavior has shifted in ways that set off alarm bells in your head. You find yourself wondering, "Are they cheating on me?"

It's a question that no one wants to face, a reality that threatens to shatter the very foundation of your relationship. The suspicion of infidelity can be all-consuming, eroding your trust and leaving you questioning everything you thought you knew.

So, how do you navigate this uncertain and emotionally charged terrain? How do you separate fact from fiction, intuition from paranoia? Let's dive in.

The Importance of Clarity

When you're in the throes of suspicion, it's easy to let your emotions run the show. Fear, anger, and betrayal can cloud your judgment, leading you to see signs of infidelity in every innocent interaction or unexplained absence. If your brain is in the fight, flight or freeze mode, you may find yourself reacting to your suspicions rather than thinking through matters.

But here's the thing: jumping to conclusions based on limited or circumstantial evidence can be just as damaging to your relationship as infidelity itself. False accusations can erode trust just as quickly as an actual affair.

That's why it's so crucial to approach the situation with a clear head and a commitment to separating facts from feelings. Take a step back and ask yourself: what do I actually know? What concrete evidence do I have to support my suspicions?

One technique I recommend is to consider the following: If a television news crew were there, what would they see? What is truly going on? What specific behaviors would that news crew be capturing on camera?

The Signs of Infidelity

While every relationship is unique, some common signs may indicate your partner is cheating. These include:

1. Changes in communication: Your partner may become more distant, less engaged, or defensively secretive about their activities. Information they formerly freely shared is no longer given to you. This also includes them being more protective or secretive about their phone and your access to it.

2. Shifts in appearance or hygiene: Sudden attention to grooming, new clothing styles, or changes in perfume or cologne can sometimes signal an effort to impress someone. They may even start going to the gym or increase their attention to physical fitness.

3. Unexplained absences: Frequent late nights at work, unexplained trips, or last-minute changes to plans may be a red flag.

4. Alterations to technology use: Passcode changes on phones, a surge in private messaging, or a sudden need for privacy around devices could indicate something is amiss.

But here's the caveat: these signs, while potentially concerning, don't always equate to infidelity. There could be other explanations, such as work stress, personal struggles, or simply a desire for more autonomy.

Trusting Your Gut vs. Hard Evidence

So, how do you know when it's time to confront your partner about your suspicions? The answer lies in a combination of intuition and evidence.

Your gut instinct is a powerful tool. If you've been with your partner for a long time, you likely understand their usual behavior and communication patterns. If something feels consistently off, don't ignore that feeling.

However, it's important to temper your intuition with hard evidence. Look for patterns of behavior that align with the signs of infidelity. Keep a record of concrete examples that support your suspicions.

The Importance of Communication

If you feel that you have enough evidence to warrant a conversation, approach it carefully. Accusations and attacks will only put your partner on the defensive and make an honest dialogue less likely.

Instead, focus on expressing your feelings and concerns. Use "I" statements to describe how their actions affect you rather than pointing fingers. Allow them to explain their behavior and listen with an open mind. When they are talking, look for signals like breaking eye contact, increased nervousness, or restless movements.

Remember, the goal is not to catch them in a lie or to "win" the argument. The goal is to have an honest, vulnerable conversation about your relationship and determine whether underlying issues must be addressed.

If your suspicions are unfounded, be willing to apologize and work on rebuilding trust. If your partner has indeed been unfaithful, know that it does not reflect your worth or the totality of your relationship. Infidelity is a complex issue that often stems from deeper problems that predate the actual cheating.

Remember, your partner's actions do not define your worth. You deserve a relationship built on trust, respect, and honesty. By approaching this challenging situation with clarity, compassion, and a commitment to your own well-being, you can emerge stronger and more resilient, no matter what the future holds.

Chapter Eleven

Why Do Some (Wo)Men Cheat? (Includes the CHEAT Test)

Unraveling the Complexities of Infidelity

Infidelity. Cheating. Betrayal. These words carry heavy weight, evoking feelings of pain, confusion, and heartbreak for those who have experienced the devastation of a partner's unfaithfulness. If you've found yourself asking, "Why did they cheat on me?" or "What drives a person to stray from their committed relationship?" you're not alone. The reasons behind infidelity are complex, varied, and deeply personal.

The CHEAT Test: A Framework for Understanding Infidelity

To help make sense of the intricate web of motivations that can lead to cheating, we've developed the **CHEAT Test** - a framework for examining the various factors that may contribute to infidelity. Let's break it down:

C: Is the person truly Cheating?

Before diving into the reasons behind infidelity, it's crucial to establish whether cheating has actually occurred. Consider the evidence you have and the person's mindset regarding fidelity. Do they view their actions as a betrayal, or do they have a different view of what constitutes cheating?

H: Are they typically Honest?

Reflect on your partner's overall character. Are they generally truthful in their dealings with others, or do they have a history of deception? Some people may struggle with honesty to avoid confrontation or spare others' feelings, which can be a red flag for potential infidelity.

E: What Environmental factors are at play?

Context matters when it comes to cheating. Were there external influences, such as being in the wrong place at the wrong time or falling victim to manipulation or blackmail? Are they in an environment that condones or tolerates cheating?

The **HALT** acronym (Hungry, Angry, Lonely, Tired) identifies high-risk situations that can make a person more susceptible to temptation, especially when combined with a family history of infidelity. Over 60% of cheating occurs when there is a family history of infidelity.

A: Is there an underlying Addiction?

In some cases, cheating may be a symptom of a deeper issue, such as sex or love addiction. Addictive behaviors can rewire the brain, making it difficult for a person to control their impulses and make healthy choices. There are also added risks when there is an Attention Deficit problem or Traumatic Brain Injuries. In these situations, the ability to control impulsive sexual behaviors is compromised.

T: What are their true motivations for cheaTing?

The reasons people cheat are highly individual and can range from a need for excitement or validation to feelings of neglect or resentment in the primary relationship. Some may cite a lack of fulfillment or compatibility, while others may act on opportunism or a sense of entitlement.

The Complexity of Infidelity

While the CHEAT test provides a starting point for understanding infidelity, it's important to recognize that every situation is unique. Multiple factors can intertwine and contribute to a person's decision to cheat, and what may be a primary driver for one individual may be less significant for another.

Take the story of Sarah and Mark, who had been together for a decade, when Sarah discovered Mark's affair. At first, Sarah was consumed by the question, "Why?" Why would Mark throw away their years of love and commitment for a fleeting dalliance? As she dug deeper, Sarah realized that Mark's infidelity was a symptom of longstanding issues in their relationship - a lack of communication, unresolved resentments, and a growing emotional distance between them. Over the years, they talked at each other, yet not with each other. He needed closeness, which no longer existed in his relationship with Sarah.

Or consider John's experience, who found himself drawn into an affair with a coworker despite his happy marriage. For John, the allure of the forbidden and the thrill of secrecy were intoxicating, overriding his moral compass and leading him down a path of deception. It wasn't until he faced his spouse's shattered trust and heartbreak that John was forced to confront the selfish and destructive nature of his actions.

Taking Responsibility and Moving Forward

While understanding the reasons behind infidelity can provide some clarity and insight, it's crucial not to use them as excuses or justifications for hurtful behavior. Ultimately, the decision to cheat is a personal choice - one that betrays the trust and commitment of a relationship.

For those who have cheated, taking responsibility for your actions is the first step towards making amends and rebuilding trust. This involves ending the affair, being transparent with your partner, committing to the hard work of self-reflection, being committed to rebuilding your marriage, changing how you do things, and getting your needs met.

Preventing Infidelity and Nurturing Healthy Relationships

While the path forward after infidelity is difficult, it's important to remember that cheating is not inevitable. You can create a strong foundation of trust and loyalty by fostering open communication, mutual respect, and emotional intimacy in your relationship.

Some key strategies for preventing infidelity and nurturing a healthy partnership include:

1. Prioritizing honest and vulnerable communication.

2. Making time for regular check-ins and connection

3. Addressing conflicts and resentments as they arise

4. Maintaining healthy boundaries with others

5. Continuously working on personal growth and self-awareness

Infidelity is a complex and emotionally charged issue that touches the lives of countless individuals and couples. By understanding the various factors that can contribute to cheating, taking responsibility for one's actions, and committing to the work of healing and growth, it is possible to navigate the aftermath of betrayal and build stronger, more resilient relationships.

Remember, if you're struggling with the impact of infidelity, you don't have to face it alone. Reach out for help, prioritize your well-being, and hold onto the hope that you can emerge from this challenging chapter with renewed strength and clarity with time, support, and self-compassion.

Chapter Twelve

The Destructive Dance of Addiction and Infidelity

Addiction. It's a word that carries a heavy weight, conjuring images of chaos, destruction, and the unraveling of lives. When addiction enters a relationship, it can be like a tornado, leaving a trail of broken trust, shattered promises, and deep emotional wounds in its wake.

If you've found yourself questioning whether addiction may be a factor in your partner's infidelity, you're not alone. The link between addiction and cheating is a complex and painful reality that many couples face.

The Allure of Escape

At its core, addiction is about escape. Whether it's through substances like drugs or alcohol or behaviors like gambling or sex, the addicted person is seeking a way to numb pain, avoid reality, or chase a fleeting high. For some, addictions become a way of life. They may trade one form of addiction for another. When they have a history of addictive behaviors, the risk of infidelity is greater than in non-addicted populations.

In the context of relationships, this escape can take the form of infidelity. The addicted partner may turn to others for the rush of newness, the thrill of secrecy, or the validation they feel is missing in their primary relationship.

The Hijacked Brain

But why would someone risk everything they've built with their partner for a momentary escape? The answer in these situations lies in the brain.

Addiction hijacks the brain's reward system, flooding it with feel-good chemicals like dopamine and creating a powerful drive to repeat the behavior, even in the face of negative consequences. Over time, the brain becomes rewired, prioritizing the addictive behavior above all else - including the health and stability of the addicted person's relationships.

The more they give into the addictive behaviors, the stronger they become. The addiction also grows in size and strength, demanding gratification without considering consequences or how it impacts others.

The Betrayal of Sex Addiction

One of the most direct links between addiction and infidelity is the presence of sex addiction. Characterized by compulsive sexual thoughts and behaviors, sex addiction can manifest in a variety of ways, from excessive pornography use to frequent affairs and risky sexual encounters. Another variant is when the sex addict starts merchandising themselves or their spouse.

For the partner of a sex addict, the discovery of infidelity can be particularly devastating. The betrayal is emotional and deeply intimate, striking at the heart of the couple's sexual connection.

Kelly never imagined that her husband, Mark, could be unfaithful. He was a devoted father, a successful businessman, and a seemingly loving partner. But when Kelly stumbled upon a string of explicit emails between Mark and various women, her world shattered.

As Kelly dug deeper, she uncovered a painful truth: Mark was a sex addict, compulsively seeking out new partners and experiences to feed his insatiable desire. The affairs weren't about love or attraction - they were a symptom of a deeper problem. Mark had a string of one-night stands. She also found that he had begun seeking out performance-enhancing drugs from various sources, including online sites.

The Dark Realms of Sexual Addiction

Imagine someone utterly consumed by an insatiable hunger—a craving so intense that it eclipses reason, morality, and self preservation. The addict gets so caught up in their addiction that they engage in dangerous hook-ups, life-threatening practices, and other risky behaviors. This is the harrowing reality for those entrapped in the grips of sexual addiction, as described by renowned therapist Patrick Carnes.

Carnes paints a disturbing portrait of the addict's psychosexual landscape, where fantasies run rampant, and boundaries are mere illusions.

Fantasy Sex: The addict's mind becomes a twisted playground, where role-playing and dangerous sexual escapades fuel an endless chase for novelty and stimulation. The thrill of potential peril ignites their neural pathways like wildfire.

Seductive Role Sex: Here, the addict assumes the mantle of the relentless seducer, skillfully ensnaring multiple or serial partners in their web of lies and manipulation.

Anonymous Sex: Cloaked in anonymity, the addict indulges in high-risk liaisons with strangers, cruising for their next fix with reckless abandon.

Paying for Sex: The transaction of money offers a temporary reprieve from guilt as the addict purchases sexual services to satiate their cravings.

Trading Sex: Power and sex become inextricably intertwined, with the addict bartering their body for influence or using emotional bondage to extract sexual favors from their victims. The haunting refrain echoes: "You owe me."

Voyeuristic Sex: The act of watching becomes the obsession, fueling the addict's voyeuristic compulsions.

Exhibitionistic Sex: Attention is the currency, and the addict deliberately flaunts their body or sexual acts, seeking the rush of being observed.

Intrusive Sex: Boundaries are violated without consent, as the addict perpetrates unwanted advances or acts without the victim's knowledge.

Pain Exchange Sex: In this realm, pain and pleasure become perversely intertwined, with humiliation and degradation serving as the catalysts for the addict's arousal.

Exploitative Sex: Power imbalances are ruthlessly exploited as the addict preys upon the vulnerable, either as the aggressor or the victim.

While these manifestations of sexual addiction paint a disturbing picture, it's important to approach this topic with empathy and understanding. The path to healing begins with shedding light on the affliction's darkest corners. By acknowledging the complexities and underlying drivers of these behaviors, we can work towards providing compassionate support and effective treatment for those struggling with sexual addiction. Ultimately, the goal is to help individuals reclaim their autonomy, redefine their relationships with intimacy, and rediscover a sense of wholeness beyond the cycle of compulsive behavior.

The Path to Healing

Confronting addiction and infidelity is one of the most challenging things a couple can face. It requires a willingness to look deep within, to be vulnerable, and to seek help. This often includes support groups and counseling.

If you suspect that addiction may be playing a role in your partner's infidelity, the first step is to educate yourself. Learn about the different types of addiction, the warning signs, and the impact on relationships. This knowledge can help you approach the situation with empathy and understanding rather than just anger and blame.

The next step is to have an honest conversation with your partner. Express your concerns, share your discoveries, and listen to their response. Remember, addiction thrives in secrecy bringing it into the light is a crucial part of the recovery process.

Addiction is a complex disease that requires specialized treatment and support. Couples therapy can help you and your partner work through the emotional fallout of infidelity and develop strategies for rebuilding trust. Educate yourself on addiction and ways of dealing with it.

For the addicted partner, individual counseling and support groups like Sex Addicts Anonymous can provide the tools and community needed to overcome destructive patterns and build a healthier life. In many cases, the problem is one they brought into the marriage and not due to something you did.

A New Chapter

Mark and Kelly's journey was not without its challenges. There were moments of anger, grief, and despair. But through therapy, support group attendance, open communication, and a shared determination to rebuild, they slowly found their way back to each other.

Today, they stand as a testament to the power of resilience and the enduring strength of love. They are not the same couple they were before addiction and infidelity shook their foundation, but they are wiser, more humble, and more deeply connected.

Chapter Thirteen

Making Money from the Affair: Who Rakes in the Bucks

In the movie Gone With the Wind, Rhett Butler says, "There is more money to be made in breaking apart a civilization than in building one."

Although he referred to his smuggling, the statement also applies to marriage. Some people stand to make money from the dissolution of your marriage.

Imagine this scenario: Your world has been turned upside down by the discovery of your partner's infidelity. You're hurt, angry, and desperately seeking help to navigate this emotional minefield. In your vulnerable state, you turn to professionals who claim to have your best interests at heart. But do they really?

Enter the private investigators, lawyers, and courts – the supposed "advocates" who promise to guide you through this tumultuous time. They present themselves as your allies, your knights in shining armor, ready to fight for your cause. But beware, for some of these professionals may have a hidden agenda.

You see, the longer your marital issues drag on, the more conflicts arise and the more money these "advocates" stand to make. They're like vultures circling a wounded animal, waiting to feast on the carcass of your broken marriage. The more drawn-out the process, the more billable hours they can charge and the more fees they can collect.

Take the example of Mary and Michael, a once-happy couple whose marriage was shattered by Michael's affair. Mary, devastated and lost, sought the help of a high-powered divorce attorney. The attorney promised to fight tooth and nail for her rights, but as the months dragged on, Mary realized that her advocate seemed more interested in prolonging the battle than finding a resolution. The legal fees piled up, leaving Sarah emotionally and financially drained.

When you're hurting, it's easy to fall prey to the persuasion of those in positions of power. They may offer quick fixes and short-term solutions, but do they truly have your long-term well-being in mind? Do they consider the impact on your children and your family as a whole? Do they consider your retirement plans? Will a divorce actually bring your pain to an end?

Before you buy into their promises, ask yourself this crucial question: "Who benefits?" Who stands to gain from your pain? Is it really you, or is it the professionals who profit from your misery?

Losing sight of the bigger picture is easy in the fog of heartbreak. The lawyers may help you legally end your marriage, but they can't mend your broken heart. Once the court case is settled and their fees are paid, they move on to the next client, leaving you to pick up the pieces of your shattered life.

So, what can you do to protect yourself and your family during this challenging time? First and foremost, seek unbiased advice and support. Look for professionals who prioritize your well-being over their own financial gain. Seek therapists, counselors, pastors, or mediators to help you navigate your emotions and make decisions that align with your long-term goals.

Chapter Fourteen

Getting Back Together: Who Should Make the First Move?

John and Jasmine had been married for seven years when Jasmine discovered John's affair with a coworker. The revelation shattered their relationship, and they found themselves in a tense stand-off, each waiting for the other to make the first move towards reconciliation. Sound familiar?

Affairs have a way of bringing out the childish parts of our personalities. Suddenly, we resort to immature games, like "They have to make the first move." We dig in our heels, convinced of our own innocence and the wrongs done to us. We cling to the role of the victim, refusing to budge an inch.

But why do we do this? Fear of rejection, pride, and a desire to maintain control – are all common reasons for falling into the "first move" trap. We justify our position by emphasizing our own righteousness, sometimes even bringing religion into the mix to prove we're the one who's "right." Each party finds themselves caught up in control games.

Affair situations can turn your marriage into a struggle over who has the moral high ground. Each of you tries to one-up the other regarding who the injured party is and who did wrong. At that moment, the focus is on the past rather than considering what it will take to overcome the obstacles in your relationship. Consider whether you want to be right or be in a relationship.

Here's the thing, though: being right and being in a relationship are two different things. You can spend all your energy maintaining your moral high ground or focus on doing what it takes to repair your marriage. Which is more important to you?

Forgiveness is key to breaking the "first move" stalemate. It's not easy, but it's necessary if you want to move forward and heal your relationship. Holding onto resentment and waiting for your partner to make the first move will only keep you stuck in a cycle of pain and disconnection.

So, how can you break free from this childish game? Start by looking inward. Reflect on your own role in the conflict and take responsibility for your actions. Then, reach out to your partner with an open heart and a willingness to listen. It might initially feel uncomfortable, but taking that first step can make all the difference.

Remember, rebuilding trust and connection takes time and effort from both partners. It's not about keeping score or proving who's right – it's about working together to create a stronger, more loving relationship.

If you find yourself stuck in the "first move" game, try some of these practical strategies:

1. Write a letter expressing your feelings and desire to work on the relationship. Sometimes, putting your thoughts on paper can be easier than saying them out loud. Use the letter to gather your thoughts. Avoid sending the letter! Letters often serve as a reminder of wrongs or evidence when things go to court.

2. Suggest couples therapy as a neutral ground for discussing your issues and working towards reconciliation.

3. Plan a special date or activity together, focusing on reconnecting and enjoying each other's company without mentioning the past.

4. Practice active listening and validate your partner's feelings, even if you don't agree with everything they say.

5. Consider attending a couples retreat or weekend. These venues provide an opportunity to reconnect with each other in a setting away from home.

At the end of the day, the choice is yours. You can continue playing the "first move" game or choose to prioritize your relationship over being right. It won't be easy, but the rewards – a stronger, more loving marriage – are well worth the effort.

So, take a deep breath, summon your courage, and make the first move. Your relationship is worth fighting for, starting with a single step. You've got this.

Chapter Fifteen

What About Online Marriage Counseling? Can it Help?

Picture Mark and Yvette, a couple who found themselves struggling in their marriage. With hectic schedules and the fear of being seen at a therapist's office holding them back, they felt stuck and unsure of where to turn. That's when they discovered the world of online marriage counseling – a convenient, private, and effective way to work on their relationship from the comfort of their home.

Online counseling offers a multitude of benefits for couples looking to strengthen their bond and overcome challenges:

Convenience at Your Fingertips

No more rushing across town or rearranging your busy schedule to make it to an appointment. With online counseling, you can connect with your therapist anytime, whenever that works for you. You only need a reliable internet connection and a device with video capabilities.

Privacy and Comfort

Opening up about personal issues can be daunting, especially in an unfamiliar setting. Online counseling allows you to engage in therapy from the privacy and comfort of your space. You can create a safe, comfortable environment that promotes open, honest communication without worrying about encountering someone you know.

Access to Specialized Support

Geography no longer limits your options for finding the right therapist for your needs. Whether you are in a rural location or have anxieties about driving, this is an accessible option. With online counseling, you can access a wide range of qualified professionals who specialize in couples work, regardless of their physical location. This means you can find the best fit for you and your partner, ensuring a more tailored and effective experience.

Breaking Down Barriers

Despite the numerous advantages of seeking help, the stigma surrounding therapy prevents many couples from taking the first step. It's crucial to remember that reaching out for support is a sign of strength, not weakness. By embracing online counseling, you're demonstrating a commitment to your relationship and a willingness to invest in your future together.

Choosing Your Online Counselor

When selecting an online marriage counselor, consider the following factors to ensure a good fit:

1. Look for a licensed therapist with experience in couples work and a track record of success.

2. Choose a counselor whose communication style and approach resonate with you and your partner.

3. Ensure that the counselor uses a secure, reliable platform for video sessions to protect your privacy.

Navigating Potential Challenges

While online counseling offers many benefits, it's important to be aware of potential limitations:

1. Technical difficulties, such as poor internet connection or audio/video quality, can occasionally disrupt sessions.

2. Some couples may miss in-person therapy's face-to-face interaction and energy.

3. Ensuring a private, quiet space for sessions without interruptions can sometimes be challenging.

A Tale of Triumph

Sarah and Tom, married for 15 years, were drifting apart as the demands of raising three children and managing successful careers took their toll. Traditional counseling seemed out of reach, but online marriage counseling provided the flexibility and privacy they craved.

Through dedicated weekly video sessions, Sarah and Tom reconnected, learned powerful communication skills, and rediscovered the love that brought them together. They were given assignments that they worked on that improved how they talked to and treated each other. They credit online counseling with saving their marriage and empowering them with the tools to build an even stronger, more resilient partnership.

Helpful Resources:

- American Association for Marriage and Family Therapy (www.aamft.org)
    - ReGain (www.regain.us)
    - BetterHelp (www.betterhelp.com)

Your marriage is a precious gift worth nurturing. With the support and guidance of an online counselor, you can weather any storm, deepen your connection, and create the loving, fulfilling relationship you both deserve. Embrace the journey, and watch your bond grow stronger day by day.

Chapter Sixteen

Moving Forward: Navigating the Path to Healing and Happiness

The aftermath of an affair can leave you feeling lost, hurt, and unsure of how to move forward. While it may seem daunting, the best way to begin the healing process is to confront the issues head-on. Ignoring the problem or sweeping it under the rug will only prolong the pain and hinder your progress.

You aim to rebuild an open, honest relationship and foster genuine communication with your partner. However, this is often easier said than done. So, how can you navigate this challenging journey and find your way back to the happiness you once shared?

Taking the First Steps

Acknowledging the affair's impact and deciding to take action is a crucial first step. By seeking help and resources, you've already begun the process of healing and growth. Remember, you're not alone in this struggle; many couples have successfully navigated this difficult path.

To continue your journey, focus on the following key areas:

1. Understanding the lingering effects of an affair and learning how to address them

2. Stopping the cycle of hurt and finding closure

3. Developing healthy communication skills and reducing conflict

4. Prioritizing your relationship and avoiding the use of children as pawns

5. Shifting from a reactive mindset to a proactive approach to recovery

A Roadmap to Recovery

Attempting to rebuild your relationship without guidance can feel like planning a complex trip without a map. You might make some progress, but you're likely to encounter many detours and roadblocks along the way.

To ensure you're on the right path, concentrate on these essential elements:

1. Restoring intimacy and connection

2. Gaining insight into the dynamics of your relationship

3. Minimizing the long-term impact of the affair

4. Redefining the unwritten rules and expectations of your partnership

5. Mastering effective communication techniques

I'm honored to be a part of your journey and look forward to helping you rediscover the joy and connection you once shared with your partner.

Wishing you all the best,

Jeffrey D. Murrah, LPC, LCDC

About the author

As a teenager, I experienced the devastation caused by infidelity firsthand when my family went through a parental affair. Navigating through the aftermath, which involved children's protective services, domestic abuse, legal fights, and emotional upheaval, left me feeling helpless and alone.

Determined to learn from these experiences, I became a Licensed Professional Counselor (LPC) and Licensed Chemical Dependency Counselor (LCDC). For over 40 years, I have helped thousands of families across various settings, applying an approach founded on proven Biblical principles and neuropsychology discoveries.

As an early pioneer in online counseling, I have been helping people through articles, e-books, and telephone sessions since 1999. My work has been featured on Wall Street Journal Radio, the Larry Elder Show, and numerous other media.

Married since 1985, my wife Peggy and I have been blessed with three incredible sons. We have navigated the challenges and temptations in our own marriage, and I am committed to helping others overcome the pain of affairs and rebuild their relationships.

Contact me via email at jeff@restorethefamily.com.

Follow me on Medium @RestoreTheFamily

Receive my daily newsletter at www.SurviveYourPartnersAffair.com

The Affair Recovery Workhop

Transform Your Marriage

Are you ready to embark on a transformative journey to heal your marriage and rediscover the love, trust, and intimacy you once shared? The Affair Recovery Workshop, created by renowned relationship expert Jeffrey D. Murrah, LPC, LCDC, is your essential companion to this book, offering a unique and comprehensive approach to navigating the complex emotions and challenges that follow infidelity. With a proven track record of success and a personalized approach tailored to your needs, this workshop provides you with the in-depth guidance, interactive experience, and practical tools necessary to rebuild a stronger, more resilient relationship.

Why the Affair Recovery Workshop is the Essential Companion to this Book

1. In-depth Guidance: While the book lays a solid foundation for understanding infidelity and the recovery process, the video program dives deeper into the critical topics, offering 2.5 hours of expert guidance from Jeffrey D. Murrah. The extended format allows for a more thorough exploration of the strategies and techniques needed to rebuild trust, improve communication, and foster intimacy.

2. Interactive Experience: The video program provides an engaging and interactive learning experience that complements the book. With visual aids, real-life examples, and guided exercises, you can actively apply the concepts and strategies to your own situation, enhancing your understanding and retention of the material.

3. Personalized Approach: The Affair Recovery Workshop recognizes that every couple's situation is unique. The video program offers a personalized approach, helping you identify and address your relationship's specific challenges and dynamics. This targeted guidance can accelerate healing and lead to more effective outcomes.

4. Convenient and Flexible: With 24/7 access to the video modules, a comprehensive 68-page workbook, and a bonus ebook, "How Can I Trust You Again?", you can work through the program at your own pace, from the privacy and comfort of your own home. This flexibility ensures you can fully engage with the content and implement the strategies on your own terms.

Real Testimonials from Transformed Lives

"The Affair Recovery Workshop was the turning point in our healing journey. Jeffrey's in-depth guidance and personalized approach helped us navigate the complex emotions and rebuild our marriage stronger than ever." - Sarah and Michael, married 9 years.

"The interactive experience of the video program, combined with the practical exercises in the workbook, allowed us to dive deeper into understanding and addressing the unique challenges in our relationship. It was a game-changer for us." - Lisa and David, married 14 years.

Your Journey to a Stronger Marriage Starts Here

Invest in your marriage and your future happiness with the **Affair Recovery Workshop**. As a special offer exclusively available through this book, we're extending a 30% discount on the workshop to help you start your transformative journey. Visit **www.AffairRecoveryWorkshop.com** and use the coupon code **WORKSHOP30** to claim your discount. This limited-time offer is our commitment to your success.

Don't let infidelity define your marriage. Take the first step towards healing and renewal today, and give yourself the best opportunity to achieve the transformation you seek. With our 30-day unconditional guarantee, you have nothing to lose and everything to gain.

What You'll Receive:

- In-depth video modules (2.5 hours of expert guidance)
    - 68-page comprehensive workbook
    - Bonus ebook: "How Can I Trust You Again?"
    - 24/7 access to the program
    - 30-day unconditional guarantee
    - Strictly confidential participation

By combining the insights from the book with the immersive experience of the Affair Recovery Workshop, you'll be equipped with the knowledge, tools, and support needed to overcome the devastation of infidelity and build a stronger, more resilient marriage.

Take action now and claim your 30% discount on the Affair Recovery Workshop. Visit **www.AffairRecoveryWorkshop.com** and use the coupon code **WORKSHOP30** to start your transformative journey to-day. Your satisfaction is 100% guaranteed.

Wishing you all the best on your path to healing and rediscovering the love and connection you deserve,

Jeffrey D. Murrah, LPC, LCDC